SPINNING SIDE KICK

Spinning Side Kick

ANITA LAHEY

SIGNAL EDITIONS IS AN IMPRINT OF VÉHICULE PRESS

Published with the generous assistance of The Canada Council for the
Arts and the Canada Book Fund of the Department of Canadian Heritage.

SIGNAL EDITIONS EDITOR: CARMINE STARNINO
Cover design: David Drummond
Photo of author: Thomas Good
Set in Filosofia and Minion by Simon Garamond
Printed by Marquis Book Printing Inc.

The quote from *On Boxing* by Joyce Carol Oates © Ontario Review, reprinted
by permission of John Hawkins & Associates, Inc

LIBRARY AND ARCHIVES CANADA CATALOGUING IN PUBLICATION

Lahey, Anita
Spinning side kick / Anita Lahey.

Poems.

ISBN 978-1-55065-321-2

I. Title.

PS8623.A393S65 2011   C811'.6   C2011-905456-6

Published by Véhicule Press, Montréal, Québec, Canada
www.vehiculepress.com

Distribution in Canada by LitDistCo
www.litdistco.ca

Distributed in the U.S. by Independent Publishers Group
www.ipgbook.com

Printed in Canada on 100% post-consumer recycled paper.

For the one on the way

Contents

The Foe

One might then be a person for whom the contest is not mere self-destructive play but life itself; and the world, not in spectacular and irrevocable decline, but new, fresh, vital, terrifying and exhilarating by turns, a place of wonders.

– Joyce Carol Oates, *On Boxing*

The Foe

Face her in the glass, steamed-up.
Left foot forward,
arms held high: your prayer wall
against night yet-to-come. One

calamity among countless maybes,
her left hook
smashes jaws and levees,
batters the temple,

makes way for the flood.
She'll hurricane you off the ropes.
So: tie up the cables to the gut.
Stuff riches in your fists.

It fits you—
lowered chin, loose shoulders, bound wrists—
this new Tao
between action, reaction. Each muscle

twists in its slick warm notch,
the knee a hinge, greased
to let loose its wrecking ball.
She knows every fragile

somebody you love.
She deflects every counter and attack
you mime and mime;
you're clouding her

with *could I? will I?*
Pow and kabam
more than reflections and air,
say glass,

say bones:
a horror's on the way. She knows it,
knows it,
knows. Bounce

an untapped
wow. Duck. Pop
back. Slip, girl,
slip.

Jab

It's frank. The standoff's end,
pitch and gamble: a taunt. Shot
from the shoulder, the tightening
circumference of now. Oh

please. She's bobbing
bravado and wrist wraps. Her guard
would let in a convoy of knuckles. It'll be
a cinch, riding

the punchline into her
open mouth
through her forehead,
off her Vaselined

cheekbone. It goes to the head
like bad news, a word you wish
you'd never learned. *Whore,*
it smacks. *Bitch. No good*

cunt. It only takes one
to clear the way for all the hooks
and crosses you're dying
to throw, screw

talking things through, touching up
the mascara. No more weeping
and gnashing in the change room.
Can you take it? My fist

wants to know. My fist
couldn't hear you. How about now?

Double Cross

The first one rolls out
smooth as the white lies
she's been getting away with:
no way you're fat, those jeans

kick ass, holy Moses at the burning
bush your man is hot.
Bullshit. You see
the next right coming—

Parry it, flash,
huh? Your eye, you're
full of it, wake up, you
suck, lookit, this is no

tomboy hoping playing it
like some man will get her
through. She'll
pop

she'll stoop to any
underhanded blow or two-faced
combination. She's throwing them
at you *phew* you've got her

framed inside your thumbs,
vicious and high. Tight block
from the hairline down, not
a blemish exposed. One measly

comeback. That's all
she's got—she peaked early,
she's dizzy, she's raining
shredded knuckles. She's yours.

Push Kick

For every cross, a parry. Jab
breeds jab, kick for kick. Against
the hook, a swift, ear-swiping

block. Or bob-and-weave swerving
up with a clock to the jaw.
The battle done right she calls

art, a dance pounding sorrow
from rock, jamming old legends
through ribs, splintering

the marrow. Is that what this is,
a cleansing? A test? Which
one unleashes three

writhing heads? When
did she become
a gang of gnats

buzzing your ear?
Grunt and unscrew
an ankle to flick

her off. Again.
Her gut. The ball
of your foot

oomph she folds—
sidesteps. The jogged heart
trips

and sticks. She jacks back
flinging a whip she found
curled in her thigh.

Skip-step Axe Kick

Barefoot blade
arcing, descending,
slicing clean: brow
to chin. *Woah.* Your top

floor in two. Steady. Quick,
she's on one foot, lift
your fist like a geyser:
gush her jaw

to the rafters, bash
her temple with a tidal
kaboom, elbows and tattoos
spraying over

ribs—your heart
ricochets with every (squish)
thunk. Poor bones, poor
soggy tissue giving up

blood and salt-caked
hours in the gym peeling off
opponents transparent as rain—
Look at them jumping

ship, pooling at your throat,
huddling for warmth. Is that you
melting down her
whirring spine? Goddamn

fancy footwork. You could use
a little rope-a-dope, mother of god,
at least *bellow* before you slink—hang
on. She wobbles. She's

squinting through a crack
in the swelling—aiming—
dare her—what's she got
left to show off?

Spinning Side Kick

It calls for distance
and flair. A ballet grace.
Step and drag. Ex-nay
the nose-on-nose, snarling

like boys in a brawl. Shh.
It's coming . . . Pull on
the clammy air. Watch her fist
spin, aim,

flash. Feel the thumb whiz,
yanking her with it. Catch her
in a low cross, *yes*. Puncture
an ovary, tear out a tube. Rise

and wind all the purged
wombs, all the fairy tales
and drawbridge machinery
into your back leg. Twirl

into catapult, knee it
to the max—your red
raw foot, her mineral core.
Bam. A bruise is born. O

little eggs. Where
will you roll?

Clinch

Ugh. Here she comes all sweat
and slime. She'll shrinkwrap you
with confessions—that time she
went bulimic just to

watch her mother squirm.
The plotting, the married man,
that Saturday at the clinic: they licked her
insides clean like a yolky

batter bowl. Want some? I
know. She's due. Give it to her low
and slow: you eye
the guy who built the compost bin

in the laneway, dream
you're fucking him on a hill of coffee grinds
and egg shells. (He's fresh as a hatched
chick.) You'll smoke a joint

and de-apron the cook; land a sealer or two
off-season. Then you'll castrate
the man with the knife his
sister threw at him. Everyone remembers

the denouement, but the story began
in the barn. She's writhing now,
hiss it out: *The sister was cornered,
pinned and left*

like a sickly rat on the straw.
Does that turn your stomach? Promise
you'll never tell. Pinkie
swear. Stick a needle

in your eye. Say Uncle.
Come on. Say it.
That's it. Good
girl.

Uppercut (Hallelujah)

Her wrist circles
the ledge shading
your neck's narrow channels,
that wishbone V

cradling your banged-up
face. She's caught you
in retreat: hauling your blades
and bushels behind you,

wrestling them up the final rise,
your fangs and cathedrals,
your sensors and missiles,
your binoculars and maps. There

you were, looking out from the flat expanse
with a song pulsing, a twang
in your ears, remixing
the plains. She wasn't a herd

or a pride, any kind of stampede.
Just an unfed mongrel—
tongue hanging by a sinew—
veering into the shimmer,

dripping demons
and monsoons. Back into
the dark plateau. Hollows
churn. A boulder

jams your spine. Your chin—
before you can fasten it
to your collar bone—
lurches and splits.

The Ring

On the mat, in the salt pool.
You've found the place

below thought, through
some rope-skinned portal.

Look, a chunk of cheekbone,
flapping eyelid and greasy

mouth guard. Crumbs of elbow.
What plagued you in the old order?

Lady, way back then
you scrambled in like a kid

through a hole in the fence. Hello,
snarling Doberman. Which way

to the bed of roses? (Where
did you leave that rusty can

of bear spray?) It's so cool here,
and quiet. Ear to ground. Any second,

eleven thousand caribou. The wilderness
flattens and sways, its borders

set up like slingshots. Go on.
Load up, lean back, before

the snap, *amen*. She invited you
in here. No one else. What was

out there that you left
or wished?

Rear-leg Roundhouse

When she's most sure
she's stunned you. Wrung
and uppercut you, fogged
and sand-castled you,

pummelled you numb—
That practiced stance she keeps
easing back to . . .
She peeled you from steam, laid you

down, Lilliputians streaming
(all the victorious rounds)
out your ears. Follow
that see-saw. Haul off

and juice her interior
wholeness, her what-it-all

means. Halve her
like a seed-rich
melon. Go.

The kick that crumbles
gravestones, that ransacks

the rock face. It's all
in the pivot—your
shin, her ribs—

In one fist, her hard-won
answers. In one fist,
her thumping

resolve. Wind
her. Wallop her.
Deliver her.

Listen. Your breathing. The bell.

Clinch (reprise)

The ref hoists
your arm. It trembles

in a storm of palms and soles,
rattling bones. (It's no fight

if everyone's limbs
stay intact, if not a single nostril

weeps and seals off, if at least
one eyeball doesn't loosen

and slide out the door.)
Where is she? You owe her

this shout, these re-
configured feet. You

owe her these wrenched,
puttied arms. Find

and reassemble her. Hold,
till all the parts stick.

Men Opening their Mouths

They fill me with bass and twang,
ale and clay. They ruin me
for silence. Their low talk
keeps furnaces up and down the block
humming through the night—a depth of sound
for every ache or want.
Who polished these engines
in their throats? Who built them
out of bullfrogs and molasses? They open
their mouths and down I go,
past the tongue and the tonsils
to the bottom of weather and hurt.

Men

Are licensed for rage and dirt
and noise, forests of hair and public
scratching. They collect cigars in the drawer
beside the Swiss Army knife—dangle them
with scotch, in front of guests. They could slide
the wrapping off you, too, chew off
your tip, spit it aside, and smoke you
down to half an inch before
the party ends. Their noses are bagpipes
and foghorns. Even their poems are cannonballs
fired over moats. Whistling and braying
at the football match, they fill the stadium
with a giant, acrid, beer-bellied
humanity. They walk too fast and grunt
and fart and think the arc they can form off a bridge
is their own glorious Niagara. When have you seen one
satisfied? The world and its women
pinch like a pair of old pants. Their mistakes
are explosions and brand new beings
who kick their way out, howling
for their due. Calm them
with caresses and TV clickers.
Give them bench-clearing brawls
and statistics. Thick red steaks and vats
of verbs, the slaughter
heaped on plates.

King of the Sea

Jimmy'd forsake his own lobster license
to see him capsize. Barry fantasizes
about stuffing a cooked shellfish
in one jet, a rotten cabbage in the other,
and watching the sleek silver boat—
that's so friendly with the whales, a whole
herd escorts it to and from the harbour—
sputter like a tugboat. Imagine him
wavering in someone else's
wake. Pound the spray

up his nose. (She goes like a torpedo
but that baby can't whip around
to save her life. She'll lose the friggin'
turn every time. Knows it, too. He threw
that wrench right over, perfectly
good wrench. That's him, that's what
he's like. You didn't know him
when he drank. That was
some combination. A good decade, I'd
give it, he's dry. Not a word

of a lie.) But what of his throne
of seashells? His square-dancing scallops?
I heard tell of an army of crabs, claws
at the ready, glowering in rows
on the ocean floor. Whose side
are they on? They say even the perch
bring urchins as offerings. The young ones
hear from their nannies and poppies
about the bow-tied octopi serving tea,
salty, sure, but steeped (like ours)
at a simmer. It's a once-a-year deal,

the fastest ride this side of Canso.
The ones who don't make it aboard
teeter on the wharf, watching him go,
one hand cupping a sweaty beer,
one hand shading teary eyes. Bets wash in
on a jellyfish brine. No one gives a shit
about royalty anymore. Mercy
in heaven, they mutter, let someone
beat the fucker this year.

Hurricane Bill

Our stores were loaves of rye and wild
salmon in cans. Water and D batteries.
We rolled the green bin into the cold
dirt basement. Bought a bag
of Dutch Crunch, a litre of Coke
and a mickey of the hard stuff.
With thick yellow rope in elegant knots
we moored the house to the fields

of angelica. They said he would gust
to 160, flatten whole stands of spruce
with his low tropical laugh,
strew the harbour with dark rum and shingles,
swat like flies the tidy white trailers,
swipe Louisbourg's pretty light right off the point
and dosey-doe the biggest ocean liner you ever saw
before hitting landfall on the Rock.

Do your worst, we said. Whisk us
off to Gander. We stood by the clothesline
in our bathing suits. The first rains
pelted the siding. The pines clattered,
hang on! Cars crept down the shore
to watch the ocean chew holes in the sky.
Just when it seemed time he'd come for us
he strolled up, sat on the step and kicked

off a sneaker. "What a godawful mess." He spit
on his thumb and scrubbed. We were bursting
to remind him he was a hurricane—
As the sneaker turned whiter, he started telling
how last night, coming in from the Mira,
his buddy put his leg through the one

hole in the wharf. "The stench
when he pulled that out!" I tried

to stir him up. "Look now,
you missed a spot." He turned
and turned the shoe. Finally, he whistled (barely
a breeze). The rain went from sidelong
to straight. We shrugged and brought him
indoors. We all towelled off, and drank
the hard stuff down. Not one
stinking foot left the ground.

Man Tearing Down a Chimney

1.

He wheels his pick-up into the drive.
It munches gravel, casting a wake of white
dust. The motor revs as it takes the hill,
and the metal bars and crossbars that will

rise into a giant Meccano set thunk
and roll, bang and clang the trunk
where sharp-eyed retrievers have stood,
ears blown back, where sheets of plywood

have lain next to big black toolboxes
shoved aside by cardboard boxes
stained by ducks shot down, their blood
forming runnels all the way home from the gut.

The chimney: it's not his way to sneak up on it.
He won't kick or insult it.
The clanging and revving and crunching
serve as warning to the rotting, mulching

brick, the hard-baked, flaking,
cracking, weakening brick taking
hold of the house like a battered hero
on the knuckle-scraping slide back to zero.

2.

Both chimney and man have reached
their thirties, but it's his turn to rise. With each
rung, his arms and legs
become tools, gleaming—they beg

to be used fully, without restraint, and in
moments such as this, when an ending
must be ushered in before it collapses
onto a child, a dog, a car, or crashes

through the roof. The red column of clay
still pleases the eye, dividing the house, the sky
beyond the roof peak, the shoreline's call
through spruce, pines, marshes and the pall

that muffles the ocean
on troubled mornings, like notions
swept from Hades' crowded rooms—
But trees and fog don't matter: assume

a shoddy, half-blocked flue
that always meant even two
days of wood smoke might set it ablaze.
This chimney leaks, and must be razed.

3.

Hammer in hand, he climbs. The sun
watches. Bulky clouds threaten.
The woman on the ground
thinks, without warning, of their drowned

great-uncle. He lies—Does he really? Did his body
wash up? Who found what?—in the cemetery
down the shore, due east of this new violence.
Had he lived to thirty, too, he'd have the sense

to begin, as his nephew does, with the soft rot,
the south-facing sections that are so shot
they need only be tapped to disintegrate
and cascade straight

back to earth (where all dead things land).
But first, a moment when both stand
together. The man leans to listen for the whispers
of old fire vapours

in the flue (like watery songs in seashells),
or simply to establish his footing on the shingles.
She yearns for bells as arm and hammer
swing. O Brick, O uncle, O clamour.

4.

Turning a built thing to rubble is a battle against habit
and denial. *You* try convincing a pair to split
when even diehard romantics admit
their union no longer makes sense. This clay and concrete

have decades of weather and smoke between them, of stillness
and height. He plants a boot for leverage, to wrest
some pieces from the core. A phone call
must be made for the delivery of a maul.

Hours pass and clouds thicken and the man
now stands wide-legged on a plank,
five or six feet up. It sags. Winds rise. Sweat
streaks his arms and neck. It's a safe bet

black flies coat his ears. But the top of the chimney
lies ruined below him, a landslide of debris.
In the gable, a gaping. Along the seam, ants,
the dampness they desire. In his hands

a long handle fixed to the black weight he aims
at the most resistant brick. He gives it names,
this motherfucking brick, but under
his breath (the woman doesn't hear).

She gapes like the exposed gable as the maul
arcs up and in. Behind the brick, the wall
fronting the living room quakes. He tears
through space, every ounce swung, no waste.

5.

They sit in the kitchen, a bottle each, solemn.
Every brick and chunk of brick has fallen.
A blue tarp blankets the gable hole and thin wall
just in time: rain runs down it, and all

her thoughts run alike. Here's a man who broke
a chimney's back. Shards flew. An old grave
shifted. The bird was lifted from the truck's
ribbed hollow. He knew where to hit, and,

at the brink of defeat,
hit harder.

The King of the Sea Blows into a Room

Marg, lazy bugger, you're up! Who you got
muckin' around now? Back again, eh?
Who invited you? Jesus, Mary and Joseph,
it is fuckin' hot out. Don't you be coming
down here writing more poems about
these poor fishermen. Marg, if there's coffee goin'
I'll take a cup. It was all true, dear. Every
word. Eh? Them lobster? Best we haul 'em
up. The fuckin' things'll molt. No, I says to him
no way. He knows it's too fucking hot out
for that. Watch this now, she'll be shaking
her head. Marg, once and for all, this water's too
hard for coffee. And you can't get real tea
west of Montreal. But Turkey. *They* got the wherewithal
for a good brew. Oh Christ, I been all over.
Asia, mostly. Thailand. I don't go
with a plan. A knapsack. This is the most
beautiful place in summer. Nowhere
better. But winter, I travel. I don't boast
but I spent whole weeks
with guys where we couldn't talk.
No language. We had a ball. They're
so fucking generous. It's bad
what they got to put up with. I come
home and hear people goin' on how
they're so hard done by. I can't put up
with their goddamn whining. All over the world,
when you say you're a fisherman, they can't
get over it. They treat you like
you went to the goddamn moon. After
that tsunami business, I went over. Saw
them on TV and thought, what could I do?
So we were on the beach building boats, and this
reporter from *Time* magazine said he'd do a story—
But I never saw it yet. You tell me if you do.

Alfonse Down the Shore

That one's arm was too short.
Or his nerve. He backed down, fuck
the hundred bucks, lit a smoke
and drove off. The patch
at the peak of the gable

was a grey raft in a blue sea.
Late July, buddy down the shore
got at the paint. No one
remembers the ladder going up
or the wet colour in broad strokes
filling the fibrous board.

Sandy, who admits
doing the trim around the front window
that same unreal blue, has
a bum hip, and anyway was in
a 747 headed back to Ontario.
Shawn is with the coast guard now.
Ray hates heights.
Bill was mending traps.

He shed 15 pounds fishing this year,
and plans to keep them off. Puts on
his good clothes, the starter goes.
He opens the trap and shimmies down
to coddle the engine. He'll maybe
go West. The oil. Newf from up the harbour,
who sometimes has her mane done pink, happened by
to mark his ascent and the can
swinging at his hip—

He didn't tell his wife
where he was going that day. He didn't think he'd
get away with it, but
no one saw him at it.

One-legged George

The half-empty pouch was forgotten
in a pocket, slid beneath the toaster,
mingled with the mail. He searches and sifts—
see how this hunt binds one
part of his day to the next? Aha!
He sits. He jogs the bag and removes
a pinch of dry leaves. He trails
the tobacco along the length of paper
as though stroking the nose of a cat.
Then, supporting each thumb against
two fingertips, he works the casing
over the leaves, tucking, shifting
and straightening (the loss of dustings
onto the scratched and knotted surface
of the table). When the edge has been
licked and sealed, he lifts the result. A
homemade thing. It bears fingerprints
and dents: will never know its twin.

Rainbow Johnny

You were doing fine. He shows up with armloads
of roofing nails, asking where it hurts. He walks
you home, all biceps and chivalry, juggling
the red, the white, the champagne

on ice. After dragging the green box
to the curb, he hoots and fist-pumps
the evening air. He becomes intimate
with your drill. He changes fourteen bulbs

in the chandelier before they go out.
Socket sets and screwdrivers
are multiplying. The barbecue has grown
into a kitchen. In the yard, a shed. In the shed,

a leaf blower, a snow blower, and a lengthy,
tubular contraption much more powerful
than a hose. This, he says, is for cleaning
the siding. The whipper-snipper's for weeds,

and the chainsaw for dismantling the mature
maple in the corner, which strews keys
everywhere, ruining spring. He wants to open
things up, so he torques a sledgehammer

from one room into another, shouting
from within the crumbling plaster,
"Let's hope it's not a supporting wall!"
Why, just the other day, he built a library

(then filled it with Canadian Tire fliers
and video games). You want him to fix
the leak in the bathroom sink; he's adding
layers of magnificence to the VCR.

He's got enough goals and good intentions
to reshingle a barn. But there are soft
chairs in which to doze, plasma flat-screens
to watch. Now, instead of taking a broom

to the bat in the hall, you rush
next door, where Mrs. J comforts you with coffee
(and brandy) while you crane
for his whistle on the walk. Some mornings,

he stands in the driveway, cradling his toolbox,
waiting for the Chevy to break down. One
shiver, his jackets and sweaters are yours.
He'd give you his skin if he could.

Man of My Dreams

He crosses the square. Monuments bow
and pigeons quit their cooing.
A thirteenth-century sun
blots his expression.

There is no hand-wringing. He goes
where he will, by what light
angles that way. Down here,
in the threadbare streets,

he locks the moon's blank
orbit in his stare. His hand
in the small of my back. My stillness
in the palm of his hand. The Sea of Tranquility
hisses. The revolution is folly,

but no one will listen.
He went away and came back.
He slept in honeycombs and hives.
In Rome he kept one slave, and treated her well.
In Greece his heels bore wings.

I have seen him dismantle
a chicken, an illness, a myth.

(There are scars, of course, and little
emperors on his shoulders,
performing their tedious ballads.)

His mind belongs to the iron, sewer-grate fish.
His heart to the breathing at the stoplights.

When he sees the white daisies spill into the road,
he says to himself, Here. This. He won't
pretend to do it all for me.

An open book tosses on his chest, the long night lapping.
I wade in limb over limb, rib by rib.

I Won't Give Up My Books

Dig it up, the peony. Stash them, the seeds.
Find me in Barker, in Warsaw, in tears.
Watch me hustle a secret to bed.
I'll shimmy the spines, burrow inside.

News you can have. All the sitcoms are yours.
I'm off to Galileo. Down the mineshaft. Through
the wall. Nobody knows the plot twists
in me. Hold your galas, your games,

your feuds. I'm with Doyle, Szymborska,
MacEwen, MacLeod. Shelve me under
yawp. Layer me in dust. Ask me if I care. I'll
carve myself out, letter by letter by word.

Love Affair

He clings to the shingles dangling Richler.
I'm on the couch with William Trevor.

He's got Anne Tyler into bed.
I'm down in the yard digging Heaney.

When one book ends, he hands me another.
Up the plum tree he's reciting

The Cremation of Sam McGee to all the local children.
We never do dishes or cook or shop.

I float the hardwood spun by Milosz,
snip eyeholes in the curtains (that's Munro).

He downs DeLillo in the tub,
liquefying, limp, housecoat on a hook.

We litter the mattress with Brontes, eyes
meeting over spines, dustcovers crackling.

We're crammed in the bookcase under almost, maybe.

In the morning we spread the news
with raspberry jam and bite.

Reading Trash

I said so long to mystery men the day
I met Great-Nan Wadden, all four feet of her
shuffling over the shag rug to the bedroom
in that matchbox Glace Bay house, where
she led me after crosswords and Y&R,

sucking back her brinish breath. She was
ninety-three years of boiled dinners,
pale as a plate of corned beef and cabbage,
leftover, still steaming, like the racy
paperbacks she burned through,

an addict tossing butt after butt
on the floor. Curled covers smouldered
all over the bubbling lino. Dozens lay
along baseboards or below the box spring.
Help yourself, don't be shy. Go on

now, dear. I fingered silk
scarves on thrown-back necks, traced
their swarthy heroes' chins, opened
a creased cover and let loose a chorus
of unfamiliar sighs. You never got this

from Agatha Christie. Back home
I told how the top of her head
reached my armpit; the Harlequins
were stacked, sordid, mine for the taking.
Three days' drive away, sprawled

on my own bedroom rug, I lit up
one after another, hands trembling,
pages sighing, that brimming
house: nine unsolved decades,
her tiny crumpling bones.

Time and Place

Pause the player during the opening
credits, 1999, *The Sopranos*, season one:
The twin towers. "Look."
And the width of a whole cushion
(the space between you on the couch)

dissolves. Katrina. It means more
than hurricane. Arenas and murder
and thirsting masses on an off-ramp,
waiting for a fucking bus . . .
There was this guy

my friend called Hector.
We were 19, first year. His real name
was Dave or Joe or Phil—
but Hector stuck, nobody had to ask,
it pinned us like a tail
to that galaxy, the perfect

fit. When we gather and try
the shorthand being passed around
on the tray with all the beautiful,
broken truffles—

a couple somewhere starts
holding hands. One more child
turns c-a-t into "cat." The grownups in the room
lay down their shields. At the party
in Ottawa, we melt the sugar into the hot

whiskey. Raise a little *How'd
we wind up here?* It's never why
we stayed. It's all so obvious
and boring. Were we brave? Look,
just look what's happened since.

Weekend Morning Long-distance

The kids have been sick, penicillin
plunged down their throats. Now
Gideon wants to play, but can't
explain the game. That, I say, is why

we learn to talk: frustration. The lines
between Ottawa and Toronto
are thick with it, earpieces buzzing
at five cents a minute. The Montrealer

checked my references, promised her
flat, then gave it to her pal with the broken
roof. How sweet. Lucky him. Plastic
speakers smushing our ears, we trade

versions of what a flake, good riddance,
that trusty hymn. The chorus goes:
It could be worse. We're better off.
I've been reading Acocella, the queen

of revision. She rescues de Beauvoir
from hordes of unforgiving feminists
(resurrecting Lincoln while she's at it).
Chris is onto counterfactual fiction:

life on earth if Hitler'd had his
way. A lazy morning call between
friends. These interludes always lead
to doomsday. Every age sees it

coming. (Or can't.) It's like solving
the marriage from within; remembering,
while ill, an ordinary day. Slouched
in the upholstered chair, legs flung

over the frayed arm, bells
hammering (it's Sunday), I lounge
in our soft-spoken exchange, the patter
of faraway children playing in my ear.

To the Parking Lot Beside the Bank at Wellington and Huron that I've Walked Through 7,000 Times

You're no hardwood floor. No loony lake. I bisect you
corner-to-corner, dodging bumpers and windshield glare. You're a night sky
flaked with spit, gum and oil: a refugee

among the constellations. You lie between me and good coffee,
home and the 86 bus. I cross you with chocolate, chicken wraps, bread.
I can hardly blame you for that deflated Timbits box, that crushed

hotel pen, its skinless tube of ink. You're a parched
slice of ground cracking open where it hurts. You don't even know
what a real parking lot is: it flattens every kind of life

outside the stadium. You're over in seconds.
You're no woodsy path and you offer no fork.
You're no tempting arcade. No meadow. No hall.

You boast one yellow fire hydrant, industrial-strength
weeds, a telephone pole from ancient times. A sewer grate
you dip gracefully into like a floor caving in around

a weak spot. You leach a nasty film when it rains, lord
over a packed cube of earth, a political prisoner
we forgot to try to save. Every day, one solitary curb

wriggles toward the road. Cars arrive in pooling
purple heat waves. They jostle for a piece of you.
On an autumn afternoon, the bank windows fall on you,

misplaced helpings of light. I stand at your centre, watching
the moon disappear. I try not to dwell. Seven thousand thoughts
walked with me here. A few made it out the other side.

At the Bus Stop on Gladstone

Did you hear about Aaron? He actually
killed his mother? I know. God.
I didn't think he had it in him. Get
this. Laurie was in the house
when the body was in the attic.
Bullshit. He left her in the basement.
I saw it in the paper. She says don't
tell her mother. Yeah. Cause
it's not true. Look at him, he's so
careful. He doesn't want to put
his hands out when he slips. It's
cold. Isn't it? Eh? Watch the cars!
Stay back from the cars. A
taxi. See? That was a taxi.
He does the splits now. He went
to his dad's sister's place and came back
doing the splits. So what's up
with him? I don't know. He has a job. We'll see
how long that lasts. Why? He's never
worked for more than a few months.
His family, though, his mom
gives you something? Yeah,
she does. Look. You just say,
Do the splits, and down he goes.
How can that not hurt? Where's
that damn bus? He wanted them
to be like Bonnie and Clyde. Aaron
and Laurie? Whatever. That
was in the paper too. Oh, here it is! Here
it comes. Come on. Give me
your hand. Say goodbye.

Estimate

How many camels and camel men
did the Magi assemble to haul their gear
down that bandit-shadowed road?
Nowadays, three guys with wheels
will move 1,000 lbs an hour,
industry standard. That's 333.33 lbs
per guy, 166.66 lbs per elbow.
Picture the small one balancing
a grown man in the crook of each arm,
ascending my spiralling staircase

with a red-faced grimace. I'm protected:
I pay the quote. He overshoots,
I pay the actual cost. His eyes rake
three crammed rooms: futon, wingback,
four bookcases heaving, the rocker,
an old green rug. Tap-taps
the screen in his palm. The bathroom's
not worth seeing. "The usual
kitchen stuff." I'll shift my clothes
by the armful into wardrobe boxes

on moving day. They'll tape
the drawers shut before heave-hoeing
the dresser out the door; dismantle
my bed, and *voila!* it back together
at the end. And about those outfits
offering figures over the phone? Listen,
not everyone has the dining table
and hutch. Not everyone has, um,

Prufrock. Bottom line: 5,000 lbs
trail behind me attracting marauders.
The nights are long. Angels keep swooping
down from beyond the lit towers. I need
this pared-down caravan: six gleaming biceps
and a hefty truck. I'll pay their price.

Circumstance

You can't avoid setting your chin
in its scribbled bone, fusing
eyelids. Comparisons can't be made:
this diseased child, that mangled
past. Some men fling it in the gutter
when it's over. Driver's licence, mirror,
passport, mirror. I heard a woman
tried sitting on it, stomping: nothing
happened. Everyone said she was
stuck. We were all lined up
tidily in the plaza, waiting our turns.

The Girl in the Well

She's trying to tell me
she was lowered to the bottom and please
could I haul her back up? Her feet
are wet and cold. Or it's not that at all.
It's wonderful where she is. Everyone should get
such a deep well, such a long view.

I walk a little nearer. There's no stone wall
to guard against a misstep. I lean
over the opening, lowering the pail.

Most days I scoop and miss,
scoop and miss. When I feel the tug,
I brace and draw my hard-won cargo to the surface.
It's heavy. The circle of light way up here
goes blue then red then grey then black.

The girl starts to cry, faintly,
far away. The pail wobbles and spills.
Then she goes on saying
whatever it is she says.

The Fox

He sniffs the edges of the drilling,
the town and the shallows, the dam
packed into the gorge. He claims

his hut, his salt-soaked bay,
his sediment, his heap of twigs.
He kicks at a stone, barks

at a toad. He darts into pines
trailing a comet, lowers
his head to the forest floor. The dry

needle bed, a lone boulder,
the mushroom cracking the log
from within, so slowly, no

treachery can be detected. Along
the delicate lichens, he picks up
the ting-ting repeating, deeper

than any hole he'll dig. He slips
free of the branches and noses
the gate. You look up.

Care Package for a Combat Engineer

1. Items from the Curiosity Cabinet at the Redpath Museum

Fragment of a triceratops skull, not to be
mistaken for shrapnel.

Emerald feather plucked
from the worse-for-wear tail
of a Carolina parakeet, extinct
since the Great War. (It might
have adorned a hat.)

A calcite specimen chunked
with dolomite, donated by D. Doell,
who spotted it some decades back
at Sainte-Clotilde-de-Chateauguay,
where it loomed aside the path,
a misshapen mishmash threatening
to mutate. Before walking on,
he cradled it and dropped it
in his sack.

(See how it didn't blow up? He didn't
even suspect it.)

Take care with this spike I plucked
from the spiny echidna: an egg-laying,
Tasmanian mammal equipped with a snout,
beak and 18-inch tongue that whips
hideouts clean (anthills, I mean).

No one saw me chip a corner off
some glistening Chinese stibnite:
angular and metallic, tinged
black. The thing scared me. Think
petrified kindling. Charred
highrises in a heap. Rifle necks
poking through rubble.

And check this out: an ocarina
with bent knees, flat ears, a Garfield girth,
broken nose and missing left foot.
Blow a tune through the hole
in its head, tap along the eye slits,
three circular chest wounds,
the hollow in its butt—

which may give rise to a few
one-liners, maybe clear the air
in the stuffy mud compound
where you're stationed. Call these playthings
or paperweights. Whistles,
lucky charms. You

with your pocketknife and practical ways,
my better-than-MacGyver, my emergency-candle
lantern-supplier, my avalanche-risk-
analyzer-with-weatherproof-pen, who tucks
condoms under the pillow and keeps
an earthquake supply of condensed milk,
who checks the forecast and respects
the rhythms of cats, you'll know

what to do. I send you these remnants,
this evidence.

2. Rations Supplement Kit from the Montreal Botanical Gardens

Their backs were turned, so I raided
the garden of edible flowers. I was armed.
In my satchel, Type II, Style A, Flavour 1
kippered beef snack. *C'est pour un soldat.*
He's on vacuum-sealed entrées—vous
voyez? Their chins dropped. They uprooted
beds of violas and zinnias, then, like harried
babcias, tied them in plastic bags,
strapped them to my waist, kissed me
twenty times and sent me

home. Here you are. Each rosehip
packs a dose of vitamin C. Marigolds too,
but ugh, bitter. Per linden, one mouthful
of honey. Sweet woodruff's a nutty dessert.
Chicory, every soldier knows, aspires
to coffee. Day lily buds, crunchy,
sweet, dump—trust me—in soup.

For iron and calcium I enclose a field
of indestructible dandelion leaves. Toss
with a bouquet of orange nasturtiums—
or save those for a spicy sauce
that will make your insides dance
all the way back to shady maples
and me. To inflict a trance,

minty hot bee balm in tea. Lavender's
lemon zing. The violet's nectar, the pansy tart.
Carnation is cloves. The hollyhocks are bland
but sturdy. All over town
they're reinforcing wavering walls.

Live large—fling chrysanthemums
into your bowl of goat stew.

3. Freshwater Amulets

Here are sixteen pearly Buddhas
barely the size of my pinky nail.
That's sixteen peach-and-marble grins
(godawful know-it-alls) pearled
in an ancient mussel valve:
pre-Viking, pre-Hun, pre-Peloponnesian.
Stuck in that old "hurry up and wait?"
These Buddhas in your chest pocket
jostle the ammo and lip balm, shrug off
your restlessness. Caught between
this cryptic wall and that sly ditch?
All sixteen cross-legged amulets chuckle.
Please don't lend them too much
credence. In a quiet moment, when
a daydream poses little risk, imagine
a very soggy, very miniature, bottom-dwellers'
bowling match. Let each wobbly guru
stand for a pin. It's prudent,
so near the desert, to populate
a stream behind your eye.

4. Samurai Suit from the Edo Period

It won't protect you for long. Those days, warriors
were sent on parade. With each ceremonial bow, the chain-link
gauntlets and lamellar plating became prettier

and flimsier. Still, their helmets bore wings. Dragons
roared from their chests. The successful Samurai could stare for days
at a comatose ant. His garden bloomed and wept

identical yellow tears. He glowed in his lacquered face guard
like Harionna with barbed curls. Pouring tea into tiny cups,
he never spilt a drop or thought it possible. His killing

was equally precise. This is for the day you can't
blouse your pant legs over your boots one more time.
It comes with plates for shoulders, thighs, back, breast

and throat. Armoured gloves. When you can't abide
one more hour on a dirt floor, when you dream
your rifle rusted through, and wish

the grenade on the cool clay shelf by your cot
was pure decoration, I give you
metal, doeskin, cotton, silk and horse-hair sprigs.

5. Things I've Stared at Since You Left

Five buzzing cubes of Spanish pyrite.
A humming handprint of San Diego elbaite.
The green velvet crooning of Arizonian malachite.
Breathless Sar E'Sang lazurite. The blue ache
of sea crystals trapped in white rock. The fog
in the quartz. The rose
in the quartz. Amethyst
pop-pop-pops. A black-and-violet
fluorite bruise. A Sicilian sulfur
desire, bright as a dish of lemon sorbet
on a stinking Roman patio. Guitar solos
of purple creedite. Calcite whites that witnessed,
through rings of grey, something ghastly
from the slope of the Harz Mountains.
Burnt Moroccan vanadinite from behind the brocade curtain,
under the occupied bed. The sweet caramel torture
of Tasmanian crocoite. A dusty heap
of Broken Hill anglesite. The scraped cavities
of Montana's Silver Star Mine. All the acid-tinted
glory of the Bronze Age, the blood and toil
of the Iron Age, compressed into rocks
a person might pick up and throw—
The bottom of Bunker Hill Mine, where the shavings lie.
The last glittery crumb of Idaho pyromorphite.
Gypsum that forewent its hold on the star.

6. Pep Talk from the Arctic Fox

The snowy owl blinked at me. I blindsided her.
A short-tailed weasel slipped past me. I gutted her.
The willow ptarmigan ruffled the branches. I ate her.
A white-throated sparrow serenaded me. I let her.

They played right in. That's what I mean
by sly. Not just to crouch unseen
between a dog-sled track and a mukluk.
I burrowed in wiles. I sniffed out luck.

When they emerge, throw on your whites.
Seal them in your sights—
creep up on minus-fifty, glacial expanse.
(This is the part where you take no chance.)

My ear twitches: the ice floe is melting.
Do I give in by inches, go down sweltering?
Teeth bared, ears back, one paw midair,
freeze them in your tundra glare.

7. Instructions for Shrinking Your Enemy's Head

Slit the skin from crown to sloping
neck. The brain might bump
and squish. Press on,

or the third soul, call him *Payback*—
call him *Rank*—will slither out,
polluting the fields.

Wriggle the skull
free. Sew lips and eyes. Boil
till reduced by two-thirds.

OK. Stuff with hot stones
and hang above a well-stoked
fire overnight. Rest

by the pulsing embers.
In the dewy morning,
polish the blackened face

with fire pit ash. That's it.
The hissing, spitting
force is sealed.

8. Tale of the Sable Antelope

Over foot-worn stairs, grooved horns
spiral a faint call to distant steppes.
Generations since the chase was lost, bare patches
shadow his jaw. Our brown-eyed savannah
beauty, eighty years in exile, ignores
that gorilla dangling by the window,
the lion on the move below the sill.

Four hooves touch the green weave,
a white chin lifts toward the blue
museum wall. Follow the horns arcing
over that hint of a hump, up one flight
to the mummified cats (a little falcon too),
the upraised cobra and Hominin skulls,
that urn shaped like fat Uncle Sid.
Before you pass, listen:

back then, we traded in lives
like fine teas or plates. No sign
of the Bridled Gnu and Bleshok Ram,
his old companions. Did their legs, after
decades positioned just so, give way?
A hunt (the labs, the basement) might yield
remains. I'm trying to see in our trio
some lesson in diplomacy—

here, in this hush, expectations
roll like terriers in dirt. Friends
come and go. On the faraway plain
where the antelope fell, that mane
like night shot up.

9. Carrier Shells, All in a Row

See *bearers of foreigners*.
Les xénophores. This one sprouts a pinafore
of oceanic curls. Its neighbour crouches
in a pebbly cloak. Let's look open-
mouthed through the glass. Could be
these molluscs would sink in soft mud
without radical renovations. Or crack.
Malacologists have no clue.

The proboscis stirs the murk
till it brushes a sunken
temptation. It gives the salt-laden
bauble a polish, rotates, screws
the jewel on like an eye. (There goes
an hour and a half.) Deploying
foot, snout and tentacles like mechanical
arms and wrenches, it glues
the thing down. The snail lies

motionless, dawn to dusk. It wobbles
in its squishy bed, testing the waters.
I'll tell you why all this subterfuge.
In every cluttered shell, there's a girl
shoving a sandbag against a wall. A man
ducking his shadow. A baby in a sunhat
with a frilly brim, blinking. They're all

tucked together inside. I've kept
watch. Not officially, no radios, night goggles,
nothing like that. Each of your fingers
pressed neatly between each of mine
(our hands entwined in the glass), I ask
again: What do you call the fortified walls
sappers notch into place around a base?

10. Scene with Alpacas in a Petawawa Dale

A day or two before I lost you
in a CADPAT cloud outside the bus.
As usual, the black one spots us first:
lumpy head aloft, legs tucked in muck,
a woolly-mammoth fur ball encrusted
in silt, gracing her estate of washed-out
grasses. The red roof slopes to a heap
of hay and dung. A pony grieves
in a patch of shade; one triumphant lily
tours the pond. In this back-home field—
no poppies, "possum-rats," IEDs—
spring is pungent and everlasting.
We shuffle and squint. The ages blink back,
layered in matted fleece.

Black ears flutter. We cross
the ditch with a whirlwind
stilled between two hands, approaching
the idea of a ready apple, spying
the gap in a fence.

11. World-famous Photographer, Robert Polidori

When he's lining up his shot, step away from your cot.
Before him, not a snag in a discarded bathrobe is safe,
not even the 16th-Century stench in the blur of tapestries

at Versailles. On his knees in the Samir Geagea Headquarters
in Beirut, sleeves scrunched at his elbows, he plunged
into charred files. He stooped through a blown-out

wall, helicoptered over sandbags, and listened. The light
on the slack, knotted burlap sang to him of something pink
and sore, smeared over the doorframe. The song was

nails in his ears. In Havana, where jail cells reverberate
with scratching pens, he snuck into the Señora Faxas Residence.
Beneath exposed ceiling slats, he revealed a single book

(atop hundreds more). At the Teatro Capitalio, an orange
fright spread over chunks of plaster. Revolutions
were peeling off the balconies. In his fist, which closes

over many bits and bobs, you might spot a length
of wire, still twitching, from the Control Room of Reactor 4—
or four gangly cribs (long relieved of their swaddled

occupants) from the Exclusion Zone maternity ward,
titptoeing out of Pripyat. Down south, New Orleans
saddled him with drowned wardrobes in twin closets;

a nose-diving sedan, its back bumper snagged
on an eavestrough; a four-poster wrangled from the ocean's
jaws, its quilt a volcanic beach. The atmosphere

roils. Polidori's quit sleep. When he waves down
your LAV, consider the dry sunrise, the clay
hollows, the missteps marking every path

outside the compound. This pitter-patter
bombing on and on—this assassination weather
—these igniting bureaucracies—this warlord

arm-wrestle—blackmail crops—amnesty wheels—
they're just disturbances he means to trick
into his little round lens. Shoulder your kit.

His viewfinder hovers. Hold out
your hand-me-down grenade, your bandana
and sleeves of instant coffee. Call it a trade.

12. Ziplock Baggie of Seahorse Specimens

Shake it before a patch of light:
one dwarf, one lined, one slender.
The new Caledonian, the Eastern Pacific,
and—careful, she's tumbled to a corner—
Hippocampus Denise, the smallest of the small,
stretching one full centimetre from her Cyrano de Bergerac
snout, over her lumpy coronet, down the bony
plates (two knobs and a spine at each
junction), through the jovial
tail, in, in,
in. The museum owns
3,000. The curators carry them about
just this way—in sandwich bags—
to show off to tourists. They're dry; try
not to crush them. A team of such creatures
drew Poseidon's chariot through the depths.

Invisible in seagrass, they bounce
over sponges, pilings and weeds—
latch on. Yank and pull, they won't
let go, they'd sooner let a current drop them
three oceans away. They digest whole
crustaceans by magic (no stomach, no teeth).
They transport water fairies and cure the worst
ailments (leprosy, infertility). In 1990, in writing,
a scientist confessed, "Seahorses are so
unusual that it can be difficult to accept
that they are fishes." Right. I forgot.
Aside from all this, they are fishes.

Complicated seahorse courtship: the male turns
bright orange, the female pink. They rise belly-to-belly
from the seabed, grasp at a willowy stalk, and pivot
like carousel ponies. Everyone goes on about
the male and his ingenious pouch: *he*
incubates the babies. One enthusiastic specimen
bore a brood of 1,572. (If you ask me, he overdid it.)
But after all those strange fish wriggled to the surface,
gulped and zoomed off, mom and dad
resumed their breakfast waltz, dorsal fins trembling

over curly-q tails. My fondness for these creatures
distracts me. I stumble after waking to the kitchen,
uncap the marker, approach the wall, "X"
one box. I'd swim down, way down
for such intimate circlings and gentle
greetings.

Poems in this collection have previously appeared in *The Antigonish Review*, *The Fiddlehead*, *Maisonneuve*, *Riddle Fence*, *Best Canadian Poetry 2009* and in the volume *Air* (Massachusetts Institute of Technology and Alphabet City Media, 2010). My sincere thanks to the editors of these publications, and to the wonderful folks at Véhicule Press for all their efforts, and for keeping me in the fold. I am also grateful to the Canada Council for the Arts, the Ontario Arts Council, and the City of Ottawa for grants received in support of this work.

Many people have contributed to the poems here. For untold input and support, which will ever-continue to inform my efforts, I fiercely cling to Lesley Buxton, Una McDonnell and Dilys Leman. For their sharp eyes and minds I bow down to Rob Winger, Matthew Holmes, Triny Finlay, Aislinn Hunter, Paul Tyler, Asa Boxer, and the members of the Ottawa Poetry Group. I also thank: my parents, who have always managed to help me believe this work matters; Shawn Lahey, for, as a start, his fearless, chimney-toppling talents; Bill Lahey for his humour, his immeasurable care and generosity, and his remarkably spotless sneakers; and Natasha Henderson for many galvanizing poetry and art discussions while on the run in Parc Lafontaine. For his lengthy, controversial rein as "King of the Sea" and his spirited heckling, I (God help me) commend Seymour Forgeron. Special mention to the folks at Therien Jiu-Jitsu and Kickboxing in Ottawa, who for a few blessed years made me believe I might actually learn to fight; to the curators at the Redpath Museum in Montreal, who create such thoughtful, enthralling exhibits; and to biologist Sara Lourie, keeper of the seahorses, staff at Project Seahorse and the editors at *Reader's Digest* magazine, who facilitated further research and writing on these fascinating creatures. My hard-nosed yet elegant editor, and dear friend, Carmine Starnino, deserves far more credit and gratitude than I can possibly offer him in this life. And to (Cpt.) Tom Good, who "went away and came back," thank you for walking with me into hurricanes and other memorable places.

Signal
EDITIONS

Carmine Starnino, Editor
Michael Harris, Founding Editor

THE LONG COLD GREEN EVENINGS OF SPRING Elisabeth Harvor
FAULT LINE Laura Lush
WHITE STONE: THE ALICE POEMS Stephanie Bolster
KEEP IT ALL Yves Boisvert (Translated by Judith Cowan)
THE GREEN ALEMBIC Louise Fabiani
THE ISLAND IN WINTER Terence Young
A TINKERS' PICNIC Peter Richardson
SARACEN ISLAND: THE POEMS OF ANDREAS KARAVIS David Solway
BEAUTIES ON MAD RIVER: SELECTED AND NEW POEMS Jan Conn
WIND AND ROOT Brent MacLaine
HISTORIES Andrew Steinmetz
ARABY Eric Ormsby
WORDS THAT WALK IN THE NIGHT Pierre Morency
    (Translated by Lissa Cowan and René Brisebois)
A PICNIC ON ICE: SELECTED POEMS Matthew Sweeney
HELIX: NEW AND SELECTED POEMS John Steffler
HERESIES: THE COMPLETE POEMS OF ANNE WILKINSON, 1924-1961
    Edited by Dean Irvine
CALLING HOME Richard Sanger
FIELDER'S CHOICE Elise Partridge
MERRYBEGOT Mary Dalton
MOUNTAIN TEA Peter Van Toorn
AN ABC OF BELLY WORK Peter Richardson
RUNNING IN PROSPECT CEMETERY Susan Glickman
MIRABEL Pierre Nepveu (Translated by Judith Cowan)
POSTSCRIPT Geoffrey Cook
STANDING WAVE Robert Allen
THERE, THERE Patrick Warner
HOW WE ALL SWIFTLY: THE FIRST SIX BOOKS Don Coles
THE NEW CANON: AN ANTHOLOGY OF CANADIAN POETRY
    Edited by Carmine Starnino
OUT TO DRY IN CAPE BRETON Anita Lahey
RED LEDGER Mary Dalton
REACHING FOR CLEAR David Solway
OX Christopher Patton
THE MECHANICAL BIRD Asa Boxer
SYMPATHY FOR THE COURIERS Peter Richardson
MORNING GOTHIC: NEW AND SELECTED POEMS George Ellenbogen
36 CORNELIAN AVENUE Christopher Wiseman
THE EMPIRE'S MISSING LINKS Walid Bitar
PENNY DREADFUL Shannon Stewart
THE STREAM EXPOSED WITH ALL ITS STONES D.G. Jones
PURE PRODUCT Jason Guriel
ANIMALS OF MY OWN KIND Harry Thurston
BOXING THE COMPASS Richard Greene
CIRCUS Michael Harris
THE CROW'S VOW Susan Briscoe
WHERE WE MIGHT HAVE BEEN Don Coles
MERIDIAN LINE Paul Bélanger (Translated by Judith Cowan)
THE ID KID Linda Besner
SKULLDUGGERY Asa Boxer
SPINNING SIDE KICK Anita Lahey
GIFT HORSE Mark Callanan

 Véhicule Press